The Floating Jungle

Written and Illustrated by

John Ryan

One day, gloomy Mr and Mrs Shem came to Mr Noah looking very worried. 'We've been on the Ark for a long time now,' said Shem, 'and we're beginning to run short of food for the animals.' 'Don't worry son,' answered Mr Noah,

'we'll have to grow some more food here on board the Ark. It'll be easy, won't it, Mrs Noah?'

Now luckily Mrs Noah was very fond of gardening. She had brought all sorts of plants and seedlings on board.

So Mr Noah's second son Ham, who was the Ark's carpenter, set to work to make lots of window boxes and tubs. Jaffet the youngest son and his friend Jannet helped him.

So did their pet baby crocodile, Crockle. He shouldn't have been on the Ark at all because there were already two perfectly good (or bad) crocodiles on board.

Then the whole family helped to lay out tubs and boxes full of earth all over the Ark, inside and out, and Mrs Noah showed them how to put out the plants and seedlings.

Mrs Shem wrote out the labels for everything and Mrs Noah stuck them in. The animals watched. They couldn't understand *what* was happening! Then Mr Noah arrived.

He had prepared a special mixture for making plants grow very, very fast. The children put it into watering cans,

and poured it over all the plants in sight.

'Put plenty over here please,' said Mrs Noah. 'I'm going to grow the biggest vegetable marrow you ever saw!'

By the end of the first day the plants were all growing like anything. Mrs Noah's marrow had to be put into a new pot.

On the second day they grew even faster.

That evening, Mr Noah took his hat off and hung it on a bean-stalk. By next morning, the bean-stalk had grown so high . . .

that he had to ask one of the giraffes to get it down for him.

On the third morning, Mr and Mrs Shem woke up to find themselves covered in spreading greenery!

And Mrs Noah's marrow was nearly as big as Crockle!

By the end of the week the whole Ark was covered in vegetation . . .

from top to bottom and from end to end. It was just like a floating jungle!

The animals loved it. They gobbled up the fresh fruit and vegetables and grasses.

The family liked it too. Mrs Noah was *very* proud of her marrow.

The trouble was it was quite difficult to *see* some of the animals . . .

because of the stripes and spots and special markings which many creatures have . . .

so as to be able to hide from their enemies.

Shem, who always checked all the animals on his list each day, had a terrible time trying to find the chameleons!

Another trouble was that some of the animals began to behave . . .

just as though they were back in the wild again,

and one of the big pythons looked so fiercely at Crockle . . .

that he ran away and hid himself among the bushes.

This made Mr Noah very cross.

It was just what he didn't want on board his Ark!

So then the animals remembered where they were.

But Jaffet and Jannet were worried about Crockle. They couldn't see him anywhere, so they set out to look for him.

First they searched among the other reptiles . . .

but he wasn't with the tortoises, or the alligators, or the lizards.

And he wasn't with the snakes. Then suddenly Jaffet saw one of the pythons. . . .

It was the python who had frightened Crockle. It had a BIG bulge in its throat!

And it looked *very* pleased with itself.

The children were horrified!

Then two things happened.

First Mrs Noah came bustling along looking rather cross.

'And I think I know who!' she added, pointing at the big bulge in the python. 'It's just the right size! Here's one creature that won't need feeding for a bit,' she said to Shem. 'It'll take *weeks* to digest all that marrow!'

And then Ham arrived.
He had Crockle in his arms.

'I found him down below, gobbling bananas,' said Ham. 'He must have eaten at least twenty!' So then of course the children were very relieved. But Mrs Noah said 'I think we've had enough of the jungle. That python's just swallowed my champion marrow!' 'And the animals have started fighting,' said Mr Noah.

'I quite agree with you. So we'll collect all the food that's left and tidy up the Ark and get everything shipshape again.'

And that's just what they did. Some gathered the harvest and stacked it and stored it . . .

and others cut down the vegetation for fire-wood and bedding for the animals.

They made a haystack and a compost heap.

And at last everything was back to normal again . . .

only the animals all looked fatter than they had been . . .

and the fattest of all was Crockle!